DAVID
HUME

by

MONTGOMERY BELGION

PUBLISHED FOR
THE BRITISH COUNCIL
AND THE NATIONAL BOOK LEAGUE
BY LONGMANS, GREEN & CO.

LONGMANS, GREEN & CO. LTD.
48 Grosvenor Street, London, W.1

*Associated companies, branches and
representatives throughout the world*

First Published 1965
© Montgomery Belgion 1965

Printed in Great Britain
F. Mildner & Sons, London, E.C.1

CONTENTS

NOTE: For information or references I wish to thank Sir Herbert Read, Mr. Huntington Cairns, and the Rev. Professor Dr. R. Gregor Smith; I also wish to thank Mr. J. S. Burdon and the staff of Kettering public library for obtaining books for me and getting the loan of them extended by the National Central Library.

¶David Hume was born in 1711. He died on 25 August 1776.

192

DAVID HUME

D AVID HUME—*'le bon David'*—lived from 1711 to 1776, and was the last great British philosopher. He completed the trio which he forms with John Locke (1632-1704), author of *An Essay concerning Human Understanding* (1690), and George Berkeley, Bishop of Cloyne (1684-1753), author of *The Principles of Human Knowledge* (1710 and 1713), and he was greater than they: he went deeper. Sir Leslie Stephen (1832-1904) wrote in 1876:

> Between the years 1739 and 1752 David Hume published philosophical speculations destined, by the admission of friends and foes, to form a turning point in the history of thought.

What Hume did was simply to show that the boundaries between knowledge and belief do not run where it was supposed they did. But for his acumen modern psychology is hardly to be imagined. He is of course the heir of Locke and Berkeley—he too is preoccupied with 'knowledge' and with 'human understanding'—but in addition he has affinities with the leading mediaeval Nominalists, notably William of Ockham (1270-1347). Most of what is negative in his teaching regarding religion and metaphysics has come to be adopted unawares by the masses who have never heard his name. In these islands the literate among us have on the whole preferred Locke. In view of the capital importance of what Hume points out, this may seem curious. He had no disciples, but his legacy did not go unclaimed. It passed to Germany, where it was cultivated and made to fructify as much as the times would allow. There is no doubt regarding the greatness of this last of the great British philosophers, but his philosophical achievement remains subtle and elusive.

Hume added to his complexity in being versatile. He was not only a philosopher. In the catalogue of the British Museum library he is distinguished from another of the same

name by being called 'David Hume the Historian'. Certainly
he achieved greatness and celebrity with his *History of
England*. His essays—moral, economic, and political—are
also remarkable. His chief ambition was indeed to be a good
writer. The *History of England* was the first history in
English to have high literary merit. As late as 1885 the
erudite George Saintsbury (1845-1933) paid tribute to it.
By then there had been other notable histories in English,
Macaulay's, and John Richard Green's *History of the English
People*, and Froude's *History of England from the Fall of
Wolsey;* yet Saintsbury pronounces that Hume's is still the
best written. In the introduction to his *Specimens of English
Prose*, he declares:

> We shall never have a greater historian in style as well as in matter
> than Gibbon; in style at least we have not yet beaten Hume, though
> there has been more than a century to do it in.

The writing may be summed up as lucid, direct, simple, and
elegant. The author felt that the subject was suited to every
capacity, and so 'I composed it', he writes, '*ad populum* as
well as *ad clerum*'. He is content to arouse and sustain the
interest of the reader, and at the same time as he tries to
enter into the individual situation of each of a succession of
selected historical personages he succeeds in being objective
and impartial. It has of course been pointed out more than
once that since his day history has become 'scientific', and is
now based scrupulously on documents (he deliberately uses
no state papers). What is the gain to the general reader? I
was looking at a recently published popular history of
England, and regarding the House of Stuart I found that on
two cardinal matters Hume is more definite than the
twentieth-century historian: to Charles I he is more fair,
and he refuses the benefit of the doubt to Mary Queen of
Scots.

For a writer to expound attractively political and economic theories and principles is even more remarkable than

for him to write good narrative. Hume does both. Unlike philosophy, economics is a progressive science, and the student goes to the latest additions to its literature. Yet so winning is Hume's style that for many years ordinary readers continued to go to his essays for pleasure. He deserves to be called the founder of political economy. Without him his friend and junior, Adam Smith (1723-1790), who is regarded as the first great British economist, could hardly have produced his famous book, *The Wealth of Nations* (1776). As this came in its turn to be superseded, so with its publication Hume's scattered essays on the same subject tended towards eclipse. But they nevertheless continued to be read for their own sake. Here is what J. H. Burton wrote about them in 1846 in his *Life and Correspondence of David Hume* (he refers particularly to the volume entitled *Political Discourses*):

These Discourses are in truth the cradle of political economy; and much as that science has been investigated and expounded in later times, these earliest, shortest, and simplest developments of its principles are still read with delight even by those who are masters of all the literature of this great subject. But they possess a quality which more elaborate economists have striven after in vain, in being a pleasing object of study not only to the initiated, but to the ordinary popular reader.

By now it will be credible that Hume was the first author in England to make writing really pay. A younger son, he did not have to face the world entirely dependent on what he could earn. But his income at the start was only about £40 a year (say, £400 today). He made repeated efforts to eke out this by taking employment, and ultimately retired with a royal pension of £400 a year. In addition, he had some investments. But by 1769 it was what he calls copy-money, and we call royalties, that provided the bulk of his income, so that he then had altogether £1,000 a year. Dr. Samuel Johnson (1709-1784) wrote more for book-sellers, but he did not make as much money. From the

History of England, all rights in which were disposed of,
Hume obtained £4,090.

Even to set out philosophical arguments was something
that he came to be able to do with felicity, thanks to perti-
nacity and hard work. In his youth he talked exactly like
what he was: a Lowland Scot. He passed through the
University of Edinburgh with his speech unpurified, but
formed there his lifelong liking for the Latin classics. He
graduated, as was then usual, at fifteen. It was by self-tuition
that he came to write an English free of dialect. He constantly
strove to eliminate Scotticisms, and compiled and published
a list of them. The means whereby he was going to change
the course of human thought was his first book, *A Treatise of
Human Nature*. Upon its publication nobody would have
forecast its future celebrity. Confident that he had important
things to say, Hume retired to the French provinces from
1734 to 1737 specially in order to write it. Yet, when the
first two volumes came out in 1739, they *'fell'*, in his own
famous phrase, *'dead-born from the press;* without reaching
such distinction as even to excite a murmur among the
zealots'. The third and last volume which followed in 1740
fared no better. He was not yet thirty. He came to feel that
he had begun too young. He decided to recast his ideas in a
simpler form. He took great pains to make his philosophy
intelligible to the general reader. In 1748 he issued a new
version of Book I. It was called *Philosophical Essays concerning
Human Understanding*, but in later editions the title was
changed and the name *Enquiry* substituted for 'Philosophical
Essays'. In 1751 he followed the recast version of Book I of
the *Treatise* with one of Book III. He called this, *Enquiry
concerning the Principles of Morals*. He regarded it as, 'of all my
writings, historical, philosophical, or literary, incomparably
the best'. Contrasting the distance travelled in point of
style between the *Treatise* and this second *Enquiry*, Hume's
nineteenth-century editor, T. H. Grose, remarks:

The style of the Treatise is indeed immature, but it reveals the ten-

dencies which were ripened by incessant labour, until Hume was the one
master of philosophic English.

Only in F. H. Bradley (1846-1924) has English philosophy
had a prose writer worthy of being put by the side of Hume.

To judge by the writings now in print, Hume survives as
a sceptic in religion, an economist, and a moral, political,
and epistemological philosopher. As philosophy is not a
progressive study, some individual contributors to it have a
good prospect of speaking to every successive generation,
and Plato's *Republic*, Aristotle's *Nicomachean Ethics*, continue
available in popular translations. But not every philosopher
remains relevant. Father Frederick Copleston, S.J., remarks
in Volume IV of his *History of Philosophy*: 'Hume is a living
thinker in the sense that Spinoza is not.' Although Hume is
so important, he had no direct disciples, but many an
English philosopher after him, from John Stuart Mill (1806-
1873) to Bertrand Russell (b. 1872), is, in one or more
respects, simply a minor Hume. Those philosophers fall into
mistakes which Hume is held to have made first. Mill felt
too superior to stick his nose inside the *Treatise;* not the
author was thereby the loser.

I

If Hume had no direct disciples as a philosopher, he was
taken as literary model by a number of later Scottish writers.
But his writings have an essence which these literary pupils
never distil for themselves. He reflects with his pen his
attractive character. He may have been inclined to irasci-
bility in youth, but once adult he became equable, cheerful
and sanguine, and such remained his disposition. He says:

I was ever more disposed to see the favourable than the unfavourable
side of things, a turn of mind which it is more happy to possess than to
be born to an estate of ten thousand a year.

He had a sense of fun, he liked old claret, he was kind-hearted, even generous; he over-estimated the abilities of some of his friends. His living qualities are all in his prose. Of him it is particularly true that *le style, c'est l'homme même.*

We today are in a better position to know about Hume's life than our fathers were, for in recent years there have been new biographies and fresh collections of letters. In 1931 came Mr. J. Y. T. Greig's *David Hume;* in 1932 the same writer's collection in two volumes of the admirably edited *The Letters of David Hume;* in 1954, first, R. Klibansky and E. C. Mossner's *New Letters of David Hume,* and then *The Life of David Hume* by E. C. Mossner. The bare biographical facts were supplied by Hume himself in a short account written six months before his death.

Hume's family was a branch of the Earl of Home's. His father died while he was an infant. He was born in Edinburgh, but grew up in Berwickshire. Life in the Scottish countryside was then primitive and bare. When he found himself with a small income and a strong inclination to study and to write, he was already inured to frugality.

As late as 1748, when he was thirty-seven, he still had to practise economy. In Edinburgh, then, having gone to live in that city, and 'having a fine coat', he was invited out to dinner four or five times a week. It was the custom to tip one's host's servants, and he could not afford to do so. It is reported that his amiability compensated them enough.

How often do English people exclaim 'There we are!' As they quote Shakespeare unawares, few realize that this is a quotation from Hume. The *History of England* came out volume by volume from 1754 to 1761. In 1763, Hume began his second stay in France. He went to Paris as secretary of the British embassy, and by then the book was as well known in France (in translation) as it was at home. In the course of reviewing the French version of Volume I, Voltaire (1694-1778), himself an expert in the writing of history, remarks:

Nothing can be added to the fame of this *History,* perhaps the best ever written in any language. . . . Mr. Hume, in his *History*, is neither parliamentarian, nor royalist, nor Anglican, nor Presbyterian—he is simply judicial.

The moment Hume arrived at Paris he discovered that he was a celebrity. During the twenty-eight months of his stay he was adulated without respite. He was presented to the Dauphin and his three sons—each one to be a king. He became '*le bon David*'. He was a favourite with some of the ladies who ran a *salon*. Even the blind Marquise du Deffand, who was cross with him for visiting her former companion, Julie de Lespinasse (who now had a rival *salon*), had enough affection for him to refer to him by a nickname. For her, he was *le paysan*. Madame Geoffrin, chaffing him about playing the coxcomb, calls him '*mon gros Drôle*'. He was in constant demand for parties and for the opera. One evening he was asked to join in a kind of charade, and was placed on a settee between two dazzling young houris, to whom he was bidden to pay passionate court. He never married, but he was not without experience of laying siege to a woman's heart, and yet now he was tongue-tied. After a long pause, all he managed to stammer was: '*Ah, mes demoiselles, nous voilà!* . . . *Ah, nous voilà ici!*'

This abysmal histrionic failure affected his popularity in Paris not at all. The failure was accepted as he himself had been accepted—with his lumbering frame, his occasional vacuous look which was to frighten Rousseau, and the atrocious Scottish accent with which he spoke French. In the eyes of Paris he continued uninterruptedly to be '*le bon David*'. It should have been as blissful as Bottom wound in Titania's arms.

Earlier in 1763, before Hume went to Paris, the Rev. Thomas Reid (1710-1796), founder of the 'common sense' school of philosophy in these islands, showed him the MS. of a forthcoming book in which he describes Hume's 'principles' as 'the common ones', and declares that in being coherently developed they exhibit 'their futility'. Hume took this with good humour. In returning the MS., he drew attention to a mistake Reid had made in English. He went on:

> If you have been able to clear up these abstruse and important subjects, instead of being mortified, I shall be so vain as to pretend to a share of the praise; and shall think that *my errors*, by having at least some coherence, had led you to make a more strict review of my principles, which were the *common ones*, and to perceive *their futility*.

There was but one man whose presence, it is said, he would not tolerate in the same room, a man who had rudely attacked him, without producing evidence, for his not exonerating Mary Queen of Scots in the murder of Darnley. He could be amused by Thomas Reid, but Reid's fellow-critic, James Beattie (1735-1803), and the latter's *Essay on the Nature and Immutability of Truth* (1770), led him to write to his bookseller or publisher in 1775, that he had just drawn up 'a compleat answer to Dr. Reid and to that bigoted silly fellow, Beattie'. It was only a short note or 'advertisement'. If he was normally equable, it was not that he lacked spirit.

He had his share of vicissitudes. In 1745 a young marquis who had read some of his essays wrote inviting him to come and live with him as tutor. In his readiness to take employment so as to improve his finances, he accepted, and then discovered that the marquis was mad and that he was to be less a tutor than a keeper. He had cannily obtained a contract, and under it he was owed, when he left, £75. To recover this sum took him fifteen years. But he persisted till he obtained it.

In 1754 the first volume of the *History* was brought out by a Scottish bookseller who had gone to London. An association or conger of London booksellers put the book under ban, and in a twelvemonth not forty-five copies were sold. Happily, in the end, a London bookseller bought up the unsold copies.

On leaving Paris at the beginning of 1766 he was persuaded to take Jean Jacques Rousseau (1712-1778), then a fugitive from French justice on account of the *Émile* and the *Contrat Social*, to England with him. He set up Rousseau in a country house in Staffordshire with servants and board, for all of which Rousseau was to pay only £30 a year. From George III also he obtained for Rousseau a pension of £100 a year. Rousseau composed the second part of the *Confessions* during this time. Some months later, however, he suddenly wrote to Hume out of the blue accusing him of conspiring to ruin him. Not surprisingly, the sudden attack made Hume rather lose his head. In his letters describing the incident, he calls Rousseau 'a monster' and 'the blackest and most atrocious villain that ever disgraced human nature'; he refers to 'the lying, the ferocity of the rascal'. Both in Paris and London he published 'a succinct account' of the circumstances. It was more than they warranted, and inflicted additional cruelty upon poor Rousseau, who had told him how he was persecuted in Switzerland the year before, but not about what had been attempted against him earlier in France.[1]

In the spring of 1775, Hume was stricken with a disease which had been fatal to his mother. A few months before he died he received from his friend Edward Gibbon (1737-1794) Volume I of the *Decline and Fall of the Roman Empire*, and at about the same time, from Adam Smith, the newly published *Wealth of Nations*. Gibbon was much pleased with Hume's letter of thanks. He notes in *Memoirs of my Life and Writings:* 'A letter from Mr. Hume overpaid the labour of ten years.' And then he prints the letter.

Hume died on 25 August 1776. In the following November Adam Smith wrote to William Strahan, Hume's bookseller, a letter describing his last illness. 'His cheerfulness never abated. . . . He continued to divert himself, as usual, with correcting his own works for a new edition.' Smith recalls further 'the extreme gentleness of his nature', which 'never

[1] Cf. F. Macdonald, *La Légende de Jean-Jacques Rousseau rectifiée, d'après une nouvelle critique*, Paris (1909). F. G. Green, *J. J. Rousseau* (1955), has a long account of his relations with Hume, pp. 331-42.

weakened either the firmness of his mind, or the steadiness of his resolutions. His constant pleasantry was the genuine effusion of good nature.'

Such was the man, but not the whole man. He had set himself up in opposition to what in Britain far more than in France was still the current trend. Most of his life he was conscious of being baulked and frustrated. He was confronted with what seemed to be an intangible obstacle. I shall go into this more definitely in Section V below. But the trouble was, for better for worse, in the man himself. As Norman Kemp Smith says in the introduction to *Hume's Dialogues concerning Natural Religion* (1937), allowance has to be made for the defects of Hume's qualities, 'characteristic of his time as well as of himself', and for his limitations of interest and of insight. Not for him, I am sure, to attend, say, a performance of Handel's *Messiah* (composed when he was a boy), to hear the air sung, 'I know that my Redeemer liveth', and then, as the strings take up the air, to burst into tears. No; and not for him either to be affected by the line:

Why, all the souls that were were forfeit once.

It is not that he was cold and insensitive; his emotions had other springs. This needs to be recognized.

In discussing the writings, I shall begin with the *History of England;* then pass to the *Essays Moral and Political* and the *Political Discourses;* next, reach the *Treatise* and the *Enquiries;* and conclude with the *Four Dissertations* and the posthumous *Dialogues concerning Natural Religion.*

II

There is no need to ransack the arcana of Hume's philosophy in order to find a motive for his writing history. He was fascinated by 'human nature'; he was attracted to the past. When he defines the purpose of history in the *Treatise* or in the *Enquiries*, he theorizes; once he settled to being a historian he had to be practical. It was enough that he had an opportunity of writing as well as he was able, for an evident purpose. Narrative can be the easiest kind of reading, especially narrative upon which pains have been lavished. That is all that was required to make him undertake the *History of England*. The work is 'philosophical' only in the sense that Gibbon has in mind when, in his autobiography, he reflects on the merits of Hume's first volume: 'The calm philosophy, the careless, inimitable beauties often forced me to close the volume with a mixed sensation of delight and despair.'

The immediate event that led Hume to set to work was his election in 1752 to be librarian of the Faculty of Advocates in Edinburgh, which gave him the run of 30,000 volumes. The appointment did not long remain agreeable, following in that respect the course of earlier ones, but by the time he wanted to be rid of it he was fully embarked on his task. Later he bought the books he needed.

He began his *History* with the union of the two kingdoms and carried the first volume to the Battle of Newbury. It was, he says, 'an epoch when, I thought, the misrepresentation of faction began chiefly to take place'. (I should mention that, for him, 'faction' is a synonym of 'political party'.) He says:

I thought, that, I was the only historian, that had at once neglected present power, interest, and authority, and the cry of popular prejudices; and as the subject was suited to every capacity, I expected proportional applause.

The first volume appeared in 1754, and even without the London booksellers' boycott to make matters worse, there would have been none of the applause he expected. The volume, on the contrary, was booed. Not surprisingly he was crestfallen:

Miserable was my disappointment: I was assailed by one cry of reproach, disapprobation, and even detestation: English, Scotch, and Irish; Whig and Tory; churchman and sectary, free-thinker and religion-ist, patriot and courtier, united in their rage against the man who had presumed to shed a generous tear for the fate of Charles I and the Earl of Strafford.

Almost the only praise which he received at the time for the first volume was from the Archbishop of Canterbury, Dr. Herring, and from the Primate of Ireland, Dr. Stone. He was assured that there would always be a bed for him at Lambeth.

In this first volume he can be observed seeking to correct 'the misrepresentation of faction'. He draws his portrait of Charles I. The hour at which to shed a tear over the royal fate has not yet struck, but already the king is being rebuffed by his Commons:

Charles now found himself obliged to depart from that delicacy which he had formerly maintained. By himself or his ministers, he entered into a particular detail both of the alliances which he had formed, and of the military operations which he had projected. He told the parliament, that by a promise of subsidies, he had engaged the king of Denmark to take part in the war; that this monarch intended to enter Germany by the north, and to rouse to arms those princes who impatiently longed for an opportunity of asserting the liberty of the empire; that Mansfeldt had undertaken to penetrate with an English army into the Palatinate, and by that quarter to excite the members of the evangelical union; that the States must be supported in the unequal warfare which they maintained with Spain; that no less a sum than 700,000 pounds a year had been found, by computation, requisite for all these purposes; that the maintenance of the fleet, and the defence of Ireland, demanded an annual expence of 400,000 pounds; that he himself had already exhausted and anticipated in the public service his whole revenue, and had scarcely left sufficient for the daily subsistence of himself and his family; that on his accession to the crown, he found a debt of above 300,000 pounds, contracted by his father in support of the palatine; and that, while prince of Wales, he had himself contracted debts, notwithstanding his great frugality, to the amount of 70,000 pounds, which he had expended entirely on naval and military armaments. After mentioning all these facts, the king even condescended to use entreaties. He said, that his request was the first that he had ever made to them; that he was young and in the commencement of his reign; and if he now met with kind and dutiful usage, it would endear to him the use of parliaments, and would for ever preserve an entire harmony between him and his people.

To these reasons the Commons remained inexorable.

The passage may make the unsophisticated reader more sorry for the king than anxious that the legislature should succeed in asserting that supremacy which it was to be awarded by Locke in his *Second Treatise of Civil Government* half a century later. That will testify to the quality of Hume's narrative, and of course Locke's description of royal absolutism in England is a travesty.

The remaining volumes of the *History* were all published in London. The second came out two years after the first, in 1756. It covered the period from the death of Charles I to the Revolution of 1688. This time Hume, he himself says, gave 'less displeasure to the Whigs', and the instalment was better received. 'It not only rose of itself, but helped to buoy up its unfortunate brother.' Volumes III and IV, dealing with the House of Tudor, were published in 1759, and the last two volumes, which traced the history of Britain from the invasion of Julius Caesar to the Battle of Bosworth in 1485, followed in 1761. A feature of these are the two appendices, one on Anglo-Saxon government and manners, and a second on feudal law and Anglo-Norman government.

In March of that same year, 1761, a letter reached Hume at Edinburgh from the Comtesse de Boufflers (1725-1800) in France. She was a lady of whom he had not previously heard, but he saw at once that her letter was a model of how to address praise to a historian:

The clarity, the majesty, the touching simplicity of your style delight me. Its beauties are so striking that, in spite of my ignorance of the

English language, they cannot escape me. You are, Sir, an admirable painter. . . . But what expressions shall I employ in order to convey to you the effect made upon me by your divine impartiality?

In a postscript this new correspondent asked if he might not be coming over to France.

The Comtesse de Boufflers was famous as a beauty. Hume was not to pay his respects to her in person till the autumn of 1763, when he arrived at Paris to be secretary of the embassy. By then she was thirty-eight, and yet she looked only thirty, and her complexion was that of a girl ten years younger still. She was not only ornamental and bewitching. She was a wit, she was learned, she was a patron of writers, and she herself composed plays. English, of which she feigned ignorance in her first letter to Hume, she read, wrote, and spoke.

She had married in 1746 and borne two sons. But her husband soon parted from her; in 1751 she was for a short period principal mistress of the Prince de Conti (1717-1776), a prince of the blood, the third man in the kingdom. She was still the hostess at his large dinners and country house parties. How close was her relationship with Hume does not have to be pried into. He wrote to her in 1764: 'Among other obligations, you have saved me from a total indifference to everything in human life.' At one time it was being said in Paris, and even elsewhere, that he was going to be her chief friend. He was ready to pass the rest of his days in France, a country to which he had been ever drawn. Then in 1765 the countess's absentee husband was unexpectedly heard of again. He had died. At once her centre of interest veered, and now her sole ambition was to marry the prince. Even though she used Hume as a go-between to further her plans, these did not succeed. Hume remained a faithful and affectionate correspondent. In spite of her futile moment of fickleness, she expected apparently that he might soon return to Paris from having convoyed Rousseau to London at the beginning of 1766, but it was in vain. Aeneas did not

come back to Carthage. Hume was never to cross the
Channel again. Within only a week or so of his own end he
heard that the Prince de Conti had died. His last letter to the
countess, written a few days before he himself expired,
condoles with her over this loss, and salutes her, 'with great
affection and regard, for the last time'.

Meanwhile, in London, new editions of the *History of
England* had been called for in 1762, 1763 and 1769. It was
the most popular of all histories in English before Gibbon.
The demand for it was unaffected by a curious rival publication. In 1755—the year after a Scottish bookseller had dared
to invade London with Volume 1—the conger of London
booksellers commissioned Tobias Smollett (1731-1771),
who ran a literary factory at Chelsea, to write a 'complete
history of England' in fourteen months. The time limit
might have daunted a less well-organized manufacturer.
Smollett did not keep strictly to it, but he delivered the MS.
of three of the total four volumes during 1757, and that for
the fourth in 1758. He carried his narrative down to the
peace of Aix-la-Chapelle in 1748, sixty years later than
Hume's. The presence in the bookshops of this other
History did not upset our historian. He saw that, compared
with his, it was only journalism, and he did not feel that
Smollett was to be reproached with taking part in a scurvy
trick. He continued to know him.

Hume's opinion of what happened after he and Smollett
were both dead, supposing he had been able to form one, I
dare not surmise. In 1793 a bright bookseller thought that
the two histories, Hume's and journalist Smollett's, ought to
be available together. He had the combined history brought
down to the death of George II in 1760. The proceeding was
akin to adding two floors of wooden attics to an eighteenth-
century Palladian building. As regards the public taste, the
bookseller made no mistake. The Hume-cum-Smollett
History had no fewer than seven editions down to 1877. In
1880 Hume's again appeared by itself. Why does it appear no
more?

III

When Hume began writing essays he had in mind a periodical on the lines of the *Spectator* (1711-1712), or of its predecessor, the *Tatler* (1709-1711). The project was dropped, and the essays appeared only in volumes—the first in Edinburgh in 1741, *Essays Moral and Political*—but that accounts for the variety in kind of some of the early ones. The frivolous he did not reprint. From one, 'Love and Marriage', in which, he, a bachelor, boldly speaks for husbands, I rescue the following extract:

> I shall tell the women what it is our sex complains of in the married state; and if they be disposed to satisfy us in this particular, all the other difficulties will easily be accommodated. If I be not mistaken, 'tis their love of dominion.

The contents of the first volume range in subject from 'The Delicacy of Taste and Passion' to the 'Liberty of the Press', from 'Simplicity and Refinement' in writing to 'The Principles of Government'. The essays became mainly moral, political, and economic, and on the whole they are marked by the author's strong sense of balance. Notably in the *Essays Moral and Political* there are pen-portraits of Four Characters—the Epicurean, the Stoic, the Platonist, and the Sceptic. Hume's object in these portraits was, he says, 'to bring out the sentiments of sects that naturally form themselves in the world, and entertain different ideas of human life and happiness'. In the *Critique of Pure Reason* Kant personifies determinism and free will in an Epicurean and a Platonist respectively. Hume is less definite. His Epicurean extols pleasure; his Platonist, contemplation. It is in 'The Sceptic' that he speaks for himself. The following passage reflects the core of his moral philosophy:

> If we can depend upon any principle, which we can learn from philosophy, this, I think, may be considered as certain and undoubted, that there is nothing, in itself, valuable or despicable, desirable or hateful, beautiful or deformed, but that these attitudes arise from the particular

constitution and fabric of human sentiment and affection. What seems the most delicious food to one animal, appears loathsome to another: What affects the feeling of one with delight, produces uneasiness in another. This is confessedly the case in regard to all bodily senses: But if we examine the matter more accurately we shall find, that the same observation holds where the mind concurs with the body. In a word, human life is more governed by fortune than by reason.

In print today are two books, *Hume's Moral and Political Philosophy* (edited by Henry Aiken, 1948) and *Hume's Theory of Politics* (1951). But in fact, as regards politics, Hume formulates no system; he offers no set teaching. His political reflections and recommendations are delivered piecemeal, while he discusses topics of his day. He states his political principles incidentally, enriching his remarks with much illustration drawn from history. For instance, he lays down four principles of government: (1) As force is always on the side of the governed, the governors have nothing to support them but opinion. (If a government can call upon the police or the military, it must still, he holds, have at least persuaded the members of the police and the individual soldiers that it is in the right.) (2) There are opinion of interest and opinion of right. (3) There are two kinds of right, right to power, and right to property. (4) Therefore, upon three opinions—of public interest, of right to power, and of right to property—are all governments founded.

Had Rousseau and he wanted something to quarrel about, their views on the social contract differed completely. They never between them raised the topic. Like Thomas Hobbes (1588-1679) and Locke, Rousseau is positive that there is, and must be, in some form or other, a social contract. Hume is equally downright in proclaiming the contract a phantom. He says:

Would these reasoners look abroad into the world, they would meet with nothing that, in the least, corresponds to their ideas, or can warrant so refined and philosophical a system. On the contrary, we find every where princes who claim their subjects as their property and assert their independent right of sovereignty, from conquest or succession. We find also every where subjects who acknowledge this right in their prince, and suppose themselves born under obligations of obedience to a certain sovereign, as much as under the ties of reverence and duties to certain parents.

It is to be noted that this view of the basis of sovereignty is in harmony with Hume's moral philosophy: what is right is what we approve; wrong, what we condemn. He holds that justice is an artificial conception, since it is adopted, he says, solely in order to make the administration of a common-wealth workable. In the passage which I give above, he speaks of 'subjects who acknowledge' 'in their prince' his 'independent right of sovereignty'; he would no doubt be undisturbed could he see today how citizens of republics acknowledge the same right in an unpersonified state.

I said above that Hume deserves to be called the founder of political economy. I quoted J. H. Burton's tribute to the book, *Political Discourses*, which was first published in 1752, and has had repeated editions right down to the present century. T. H. Huxley (1825-1895), in his short essay on Hume (1878), points out that, on being translated into French immediately on first publication in Britain, it 'conferred a European reputation upon their author; and, what was more to the purpose, influenced the later school of economists of the eighteenth century'. It brought Hume to the attention of Montesquieu (1689-1755), himself the author of original inquiries on the subject. Among the French economists whom Huxley has in mind may be named Quesnay (1694-1774), Mirabeau (1715-1789), Raynal (1713-1796), and Turgot (1747-1781). Mirabeau's *L'Ami des Hommes* disputes Hume's theories of population. I have indicated that the economic essays were the essential stimulus which led Adam Smith to write *The Wealth of Nations*. This had been preceded in 1767 by Sir James Steuart's *Inquiry into the Principles of Political Economy*, but that unfortunately is valueless. How Hume's *Discourses* fathered Smith's

treatise is easily seen. Smith sets out from recognition of the
fact that wealth is not silver and gold but the goods which
men use and consume, and which are produced by their
labour. Hume was first in adopting more or less the same
starting-point, as he makes clear:

> It appears that want of money can never injure any state within itself;
> for men and commodities are the real strength of any community.

The *Political Discourses* remain pleasant to read, and much
of their comment is strikingly up-to-date. At a time when
three societies are investigating money and credit in Britain,
France, and the United States respectively, and the piling up
of national debt gives rise to grave warnings,[1] Hume might
be one of ourselves:

> In general we may observe that the dearness of everything from plenty
> of money, is a disadvantage which attends an established commerce, and
> sets bounds to it in every country by enabling the poorer states to under-
> sell the richer in all foreign markets.
>
> This has made me entertain a great doubt concerning the benefits of
> *banks* and *paper-credit*, which are so generally esteemed advantageous to
> every nation. That provisions and labour should become dear by the
> increase of trade and money is, in many respects, an inconvenience. . . .
> There appears no reason for increasing that inconvenience by a *counterfeit
> money*, which foreigners will not accept in payment, and which any
> great disorder in the state will reduce to nothing. . . . To endeavour
> artificially to increase such a credit can never be the interest of any
> trading nation; but must lay them under disadvantages, by increasing
> money beyond its natural proportion to labour and commodities, and
> thereby heighten their price to the merchant and manufacturer.

What national debt really is he sums up in a sentence: 'Our
modern expedient is to mortgage the public revenues and to
trust that posterity will pay off the incumbrances contracted
by their ancestors.' He realizes that 'our national debts
furnish merchants with a species of money that is con-

[1] cf., e.g., D. Allhusen and E. Holloway, *Money: The Decisive Factor*
(1959).

tinually multiplying in their hands and produces sure gain'. But, counter-balancing the advantages to merchants, 'the taxes which are levied to pay the interest on these debts are apt to be a check upon industry, to heighten the price of labour, and to be an oppression to the poorer sort'. He might be foreseeing the twentieth century where he says: 'The practice of contracting debt will almost infallibly be abused by every government.' And his final conclusion in the matter may yet be verified, for it is: 'Either the nation must destroy public credit or public credit will destroy the nation.'

IV

I come to the philosophy, Hume's chief title to fame. If we want to read him as 'the one master of philosophic English', we have to open the second Enquiry, the *Enquiry concerning the Principles of Morals*, that piece of writing which he himself regarded as 'incomparably' his best. This is from the second Appendix, 'Of Self-Love':

An epicurean or a Hobbist readily allows, that there is such a thing as a friendship in the world, without hypocrisy or disguise; though he may attempt, by a philosophical chymistry, to resolve the elements of this passion, if I may so speak, into those of another, and explain every affection to be self-love, twisted and moulded, by a particular turn of imagination, into a variety of appearances. But as the same turn of imagination prevails not in every man, nor gives the same direction to the original passion; this is sufficient even according to the selfish system to make the widest difference in human characters, and denominate one man virtuous and humane, another vicious and meanly interested. I esteem the man whose self-love, by whatever means, is so directed as to give him a concern for others, and render him serviceable to society: as I hate or despise him, who has no regard to any thing beyond his own gratifications and enjoyments. In vain would you suggest that these characters, though seemingly opposite, are at bottom the same, and that a very inconsiderable turn of thought forms the whole difference between them. Each character, notwithstanding these inconsiderable differences, appears to me, in practice, pretty durable and untransmutable. And I find not in this more than in other subjects, that the natural sentiments arising from the general appearances of things are easily destroyed by subtile reflections concerning the minute origin of these appearances. Does not the lively, cheerful colour of a countenance inspire me with complacency and pleasure; even though I learn from philosophy that all difference of complexion arises from the most minute differences of thickness, in the most minute parts of the skin; by means of which a superficies is qualified to reflect one of the original colours of light, and absorb the others?

But though the question concerning the universal or partial selfishness of man be not so material as is usually imagined to morality and practice, it is certainly of consequence in the speculative science of human nature, and is a proper object of curiosity and enquiry.

That passage seems perfectly straightforward. It is easy to agree with. I need offer no comment. The quality of the writing shows what Hume ultimately achieved. But if we want not simply to admire the style but come to grips with what it is in Hume that formed 'a turning point in the history of thought', we have to go the *Treatise* as well as to *Enquiries;* in fact, to the *Treatise* above all.

In Britain during the author's lifetime the *Treatise* was very generally ignored. No second edition came out till 1817, seventy-eight years after the first appearance of Volumes I and II. The few who tried to understand it failed dismally. Kant, in his *Prolegomena to every Future Metaphysic*, refers to this. He says:

But the perpetual hard fate of metaphysics would not allow Hume to be understood. We cannot without a certain sense of pain consider how utterly his opponents, Reid, Oswald, Beattie, and even Priestley, missed the point of the problem. For while they were ever assuming as conceded what he doubted, and demonstrating with eagerness and often with arrogance what he never thought of disputing, they so overlooked his inclination towards a better state of things, that everything remained undisturbed in its old condition.

I have already mentioned Hume's irritation at the irrelevant attacks of James Beattie. The 'Advertisement' which he drew up in 1775 out of annoyance at these and other evidences of complete misunderstanding was for insertion in the next edition of the *Essays* (with which the *Enquiries* were then being included), and it actually disowns the *Treatise*!

Today the situation everywhere is different. It may be that the argument of the *Treatise* continues to be misrepresented here and there. But, at least since the publication in 1941 of *The Philosophy of David Hume*, by Norman Kemp Smith (1872-1958), it is without excuse. Incidentally, Kemp Smith had already stated the heart of the matter in his *Commentary to Kant's Critique of Pure Reason* (1918). In both places he makes it clear that the *Treatise* cannot be dispensed with. Happily it is available today in full in two editions, and a portion of it together with an *Abstract* of the whole which the author drew up himself, in *Hume's Theory of Knowledge* (Edinburgh, 1951), and another portion, together with some of the essays, in *Hume's Theory of Politics* (same place and date).

Although nobody in Britain during the author's lifetime could understand what he was driving at in the *Treatise*, there was one man abroad who did, and that made all the difference to the turning point in the history of thought. To quote Kemp Smith's *Commentary*:

> It is a very remarkable historical fact that notwithstanding the clearness and cogency of Hume's argument, and the appearance of such competent thinkers as Thomas Reid in Scotland, and Lambert and Crusius in Germany, no less than thirty years should have elapsed before Hume found a single reader capable of appreciating the teaching of the *Treatise* at its true value.

That single reader was of course Immanuel Kant (1724-1804). Only the *Enquiries* had been translated into German, and hence Kant was unacquainted with the *Treatise*. But presently there came into his hands a translation of Beattie's *Essay*, which I referred to above, and in this he found an essential passage of the *Treatise* quoted, a passage not

repeated in the first *Enquiry* at all. So it was that he made his
famous avowal:

> David Hume's teaching . . . first interrupted my dogmatic slumber,
> and gave my investigations in the field of speculative philosophy a quite
> new direction.

The passage of the *Treatise* was essential for Kant because it
deals with causation fundamentally. In the first *Enquiry*
Hume discusses the fact that although whenever anything
happens we either assign to it a cause or else expect it to
have a particular effect, there is no rational ground for doing
so. But it is only in the *Treatise* that he calls in question man's
conviction that there always is a relation of cause and effect
between things or events. That any two particular events are
connected as cause and effect we do not in fact perceive.
That is to say, there is nothing in any particular event which
implies a cause for it or that it is an effect. Before Hume,
the French Oratorian Malebranche (1638-1715) and Locke
both insisted on the absence of anything in experience to
make us see such a connexion in a particular instance. We
simply cannot demonstrate the existence of a thing from the
existence of another thing. But Hume goes further, and that
is why he is more profound.

Even though we do not perceive the causal bond in
particular instances, we could safely assume it in each
instance if we had good reason to be sure that all pairs of
events, all changes in things, were causally connected. In the
Treatise, and only in the *Treatise*, Hume points out that we
have no such good reason. That is to say, he calls in question
the causal axiom: 'Every change must have a cause.' In the
categorical character of the 'must' of that axiom there is, he
points out, no logic. In fact we do not know that there must
always be a cause. Once the impossibility of knowledge in
that respect is recognized, a whole set of new epistemological
problems comes into view. If causal connexion is not, as had
hitherto been taken for granted, within the domain of logic,

then, as Kemp Smith says, 'its true connotation must lie elsewhere'. We are compelled to believe in necessary connexion, and of course Hume never dreams of disputing the compulsion. Nobody is more generous with assigning causes than he in his *History*. Unless we felt sure of causal connexion, nothing would be intelligible. But to feel sure is not to be sure. We only believe. That is to say, the boundaries between knowledge and belief are not where it was thought they were. Furthermore, for Hume, belief differs radically from knowledge. We acquire knowledge by reason; belief we attain by feeling. 'Belief', he says, 'is more properly an act of the sensitive, than of the cogitative part of our natures.' About causation we only *feel* sure, and this feeling ensues from custom. As he says again, 'All our reasonings concerning causes and effects are deriv'd from nothing else but custom'. And what for individuals is custom and habit is for society tradition.

The domain of reason, which alone yields knowledge, is made smaller, but the last thing of which to accuse Hume is of being irrational. He is no advocate of doing without reason, like some writers today. He is no fool. He understands that we depend upon reason as far as it will take us. Only reason can show us the limits of our reason and the confines of our knowledge. Only thanks to reason do we discover how much the individual owes to custom and habit, and society to tradition. Finally we have only our reason to set bounds to our beliefs.

What are the consequences for ethics and politics? What for religious faith?

V

Adulation by the wit and beauty of Paris should have been as blissful as Bottom wound in Titania's arms. But at Paris from October 1763 to the beginning of January 1766 Hume's delight was not unalloyed. He contrasted his celebrity in

France with the disappointments and frustrations he had met
with at home. To Gilbert Elliot of Minto he wrote from
Paris in March 1764: 'I have been accustom'd to meet with
nothing but insults and indignities from my native country.'
Something which never came fully into view had dogged his
career: it was more than the London booksellers' ban on the
sale of Volume I of his *History;* more than the refusal of the
Edinburgh advocates to let him choose the additions to their
library; more than the rancour shown when he refrained
from exonerating Mary Queen of Scots and from blackening
the memory of Charles I; more than the public's inability to
make head or tail of the *Treatise.* Time and again he wanted
to speak out, and was prevailed upon to delete or 'to soften'
his proposed utterance. But what still went into print under
his name sufficed to keep alive and active the hostility which
was partly open and avowed, partly busy in the dark behind
his back.

Why was he rejected for the chair of pneumatical
philosophy at Edinburgh in 1744 and 1745 and for the chair
of logic at Glasgow in 1752? He was more than suspected of
being religiously unsound. After his funeral two men were
put on watch at his tomb for eight nights for fear some
enthusiastic churchgoers might, out of their Christian
charity, attempt its desecration. The marks of the droppings
from the watchmen's candles long commemorated their
vigil.

Once there was even talk of taking proceedings against
him. In 1755 and again in 1756 it was attempted to have the
general assembly of the Church of Scotland pronounce his
formal excommunication (and that of his kinsman, Lord
Kames, a church elder!), and although the attempts failed
they were reinforced by the circulation of grossly written
pamphlets against him. In the same year 1755 he proposed to
his bookseller, Andrew Millar, a volume to be called *Four
Dissertations*, and when, for inclusion in it, he offered one
'Of Suicide'—a justification—and another, 'Of the Immortality of the Soul'—denying any likelihood of it—Millar

took advice. There was then talk of a prosecution—by the
Lord Chancellor. The two 'dissertations' were withdrawn.
They were only published posthumously, and then by
pirates. Of the *Four Dissertations* which at last came out in
1757, two were substitutes for those abandoned ones. What
remained was still challenging. The first in the volume was
entitled 'The Natural History of Religion'. An extract will
indicate its tone:

> Lucian observes that a young man, who reads the history of the gods in
> Homer or Hesiod, and finds their factions, wars, injustice, incest,
> adultery, and other immoralities so highly celebrated, is much surprised
> afterwards, when he comes into the world, to observe that punishments
> are by law inflicted on the same actions, which he had been taught to
> ascribe to superior beings. The contradiction is still perhaps stronger
> between the representations given us by some later religions and our
> natural ideas of generosity, lenity, impartiality, and justice; and in
> proportion to the multiplied terrors of these religions, the barbarous
> conceptions of the divinity are multiplied upon us.

That 'dissertation' on the history of religion called forth a
critical pamphlet, characterized, Hume says, by 'illiberal
petulance, arrogance, and scurrility'.

The prime mover in this interference and condemnation
was William Warburton, Bishop of Gloucester (1698-1779),
who was a man of influence. According to Gibbon, 'the real
merit of Warburton was degraded by the pride and pre-
sumption with which he pronounced his infallible decrees'.
Warburton had praised Alexander Pope's *Essay on Man*
(1733), and after Pope's death it fell to him to re-edit Pope's
Shakespeare. Of the result there is no improving on George
Sampson's description in *The Concise Cambridge History of
English Literature* (1941), as follows:

> Warburton was one of those bullies of literature whose success is
> incredible to later ages. His edition (1747) is remarkable alike for its
> insolence and its ignorance. His conjectures would furnish a curiosity
> shop of impossible words.

Such was the fellow who, being incapable of suspecting what
his actual position was in relation to Hume, adopted towards
Hume's writings a tone of ludicrous superiority.

That does not mean that his accusations were baseless.
Hume was neither heretic, deist, nor atheist. But he had next
to no religion. As a boy in Berwickshire, he had accepted
church-going and the corresponding attitude of mind which
he was later so vigorously to condemn. He had accepted
having Sunday turned into a lugubrious day by the imposi-
tion of over-prolonged devotions. Matters are different in
Scotland today. Less than a century ago many a Scot was
still throwing off all religion on reaching manhood in
reaction against the oppression of such Sundays as Hume
suffered in boyhood. But Hume's want of religion, once he
had grown up, had better grounds. It was by reading and
reflecting on what he had read that he lost whatever faith
had been his—by reading, for instance, Locke, and also
Samuel Clarke (1675-1729), whose *A Demonstration of the
Being and Attributes of God* (1704) had on him apparently the
opposite of its intended effect.

As with other apostates, however, religion went on pre-
occupying him. After he had published Section 10 of the
first *Enquiry*, 'Of Miracles', and 'The Natural History of
Religion' in *Four Dissertations*, he yet had more to say.
Between the years 1749 to 1751 he began writing a set of
Dialogues concerning Natural Religion. He revised and
polished them from time to time, and although he did not
attempt to give them to the public himself, he was anxious
that after his death they should be duly submitted to the
judgement of the world. He entrusted them to his nephew,
who brought them out in 1779.

The purpose in them is simple. One of the familiar
mediaeval proofs of the existence of God, the argument from
design, is subjected to a searching analysis and found worth-
less. Hume concludes from this in effect to the vanity of all
metaphysics.

Kant was not the only citizen of Koenigsberg to come

under Hume's spell. The *Dialogues* were read and translated
into German by a friend of his, Johann Georg Hamann
(1730-1788). Kant read through the MS. In 'The Transcen-
dental Dialectic' of the *Critique of Pure Reason* all the
mediaeval proofs of the existence of God are declared to be
entirely unconvincing. Kemp Smith thinks it likely that
Kant's reading of Hamann's translation of Hume's *Dialogues*
both strengthened him in his rejection of natural theology
and enabled him 'to define more clearly than he otherwise
would have done, the negative consequences of his own
Critical principles'. We know that, unlike Hume, Kant
insists on the necessity of metaphysical inquiry for moral
reasons. We need to tackle the problems of the existence of
God, the freedom of the will, and the immortality of the
soul, in our search for a decision regarding what we ought
to do. But it seemed to Hamann that in wrestling with these
problems Kant surrenders too readily to the rationalism of
the Enlightenment. Hamann rose in opposition to the Age of
Reason. In 1757, he had come to London from his native
Koenigsberg on a business mission, and during his stay he
underwent a religious conversion. Thereafter he sets up
belief over reason, and finds that constantly the true is the
incredible. 'Lies and novels must be plausible', he says, 'also
hypotheses and fables; but not the truth.' According to
Professor Fritz Blanke, of Zürich, in his *Hamann-Studien*, it
was Hamann, more than anybody else, who preserved the
evangelical faith in Germany from being corrupted by that
rationalism of the Enlightenment, to which Kant, he felt,
gives way. What attracted Hamann to Hume was recognition of the limits of the powers of human reason. 'Hume is
always my man', he says, 'because he at least honours the
principle of belief and has taken it up into his system.'
Thus Hume gave rise, chiefly in Germany, to two streams of
thought, philosophical and theological, with Kant, on the
one hand, leading to G. W. F. Hegel (1770-1831); with
Hamann, on the other, as the inspiration of Søren Kierke-
gaard (1813-1855). If Kant may be reproached with falling

in too readily with the current naturalism, Hamann in his writings remains wayward and eccentric.

But neither seems to have carried on, or to have transmitted, Hume's teaching so that it attained to its ultimate conclusion. Hume is under the delusion that the methods of Newtonian physics are appropriate to the study of human nature, and, odder still, that he is applying them. In morality as in physics necessity prevails. We impute responsibility, Hume says, because we are convinced that a man's actions disclose his character and abiding dispositions, and only as they do so can we give them our moral approval or blame. For Hume, the agent simply acts. Only an observer judges what he does. It seems a partial view of what happens. He ignores moral struggle and indecision; he is a stranger to the conquest of temptation:

> 'Tis one thing to be tempted, Escalus,
> Another thing to fall.

But he does hold that feeling, belief, custom are our moral guides. Even so he does not see that this implies admitting moral tradition back into its own, and religion too. For all religion, all propitiation of the Unseen Powers, are what has been transmitted from generation to generation. When he writes of 'our natural ideas of generosity, lenity, impartiality, and justice', his only ground for calling them 'natural' must be Pascal's adage, '*la coutume est une seconde nature*'. Whence do those so-called natural ideas come from to begin with if not from those gods, whose conduct, in the Greek mythology, he declares monstrous?

It is as though he was on the high road to an illumination which lies just round the corner but is brought up short by his rather pedestrian naturalism. That is the significance of his affinities with some of the mediaeval Nominalists, and notably William of Ockham. And he has his affinity also to a sceptical believer nearer his own day, the sceptical but believing Pascal (1623-1662).

Hume is under no illusions about mankind. He does not rise to the tragic view, but he has the needful disposition. In Part XI of the *Dialogues concerning Natural Religion*, Cleanthes speaks of 'the total infirmity of human reason, . . . the great and universal misery and still greater wickedness of men'. Are those words of Cleanthes' so remote from Pascal's *'misère de l'homme sans Dieu'*? We do not interpret the world thanks to our reason, Hume says, but by means of our spontaneous feelings of belief and the inheritance of custom. That is what in effect Pascal says too, but Pascal adds that it is the custom to accept the religion transmitted to us by tradition.

As for the Nominalists, Father Copleston, in Volume III of his *History of Philosophy*, refers to Nicolas of Autrecourt (b. 1300), who, like Hume 450 years later, holds that we have no certainty regarding cause and effect, for from the existence of one thing no other thing can be inferred to exist. Hume successfully disputes the validity of the argument from design. Like Kant, William of Ockham rejects all the so-called metaphysical proofs of the existence of God. But Ockham, suffering too his share of 'insults and indignities', not from his 'native country', but from a succession of Avignon popes—Ockham retains his faith.

VI

David Hume, then, is one of the glories of our prose literature. As historian, essayist, or philosopher, he writes well. He could be proud of being the author of best-sellers, for they were best-sellers of quality. He had sweetness of character, and his character is openly reflected in his writings, particularly in his *History of England*. Through the pages of that sustained work, there flows the milk of human sympathy. Among his numerous essays, a selection are still a pleasure to read. They remain short repositories of wisdom in practical affairs, in politics, economics, and personal relations. His greatest achievement, however, was in philosophy.

He demonstrates that the limits of human knowledge are narrower than had previously been assumed. By 'knowledge' he means not the storehouse of memory but what can be won by means of legitimate inference. He makes us see that we cannot know that either entities or events are bound together in pairs by any system of cause and effect; we must be content to believe it. Likewise, in order to make our way about in daily life as well as in the natural sciences we have to persist in drawing inductive generalizations, although most of them we are unable to justify by evidence. As regards the principles of morality, he makes us see that no valid conclusion can be deduced of what ought to be from apprehension of what is. At first sight those discoveries may seem negative. They are really the opposite, because they have enlarged man's consciousness of what he is and of what he may attempt. They, and they especially, made possible psycho-analysis, and the postulated entities of the subconscious, the unconscious, and the id. Freud, Adler, and Jung may have been largely unaware of his writings; they are nevertheless deep in his debt. He had to open the way in order that they might come after.

Hume had dropped religion for himself, and he tended to scoff at Roman Catholics as superstitious and at Presbyterians as enthusiasts. When his teaching filtered down to the multitude, it encouraged religious indifference. In fact, in those fields where men of learning are in danger of vainglory, his lesson is a reminder to be humble. In the thick of the Age of Reason, in an era of creeping scepticism, he analyzes man's mental capacity so acutely as to restore custom and instinctive belief to the dominant position which they had occupied in the Age of Faith.

DAVID HUME

A Select Bibliography

(Place of publication London unless otherwise stated)

Bibliography:

A BIBLIOGRAPHY OF DAVID HUME AND OF SCOTTISH PHILOSOPHY FROM HUTCHESON TO BALFOUR, by T. E. Jessop (1938)

—writings on Hume from 1938 to 1952 are listed by J. Lameere in *Revue internationale de philosophie*, vi, 1952.

Collected Editions and Selections:

ESSAYS AND TREATISES ON SEVERAL SUBJECTS. 4 vols. (1753-6; 1758; 1760; 1770; 2 vols., with Hume's last corrections, 1764; 1768, and numerous subsequent editions).

THE PHILOSOPHICAL WORKS INCLUDING ALL THE ESSAYS. 4 vols. Edinburgh (1826).

THE PHILOSOPHICAL WORKS, ed. T. H. Green and T. H. Grose. 4 vols. (1874-5)

—these volumes contain the *Treatise* and the *Enquiries*, all the *Essays*, including those withdrawn, *Four Dissertations*, and two long introductions, one by Green, one by Grose.

ESSAYS: MORAL, POLITICAL AND LITERARY (1903, rptd. 1963).

OEUVRES PHILOSOPHIQUES CHOISIES, tr. par M. David. 2 vols. Paris (1912).

HUME'S MORAL AND POLITICAL PHILOSOPHY, ed. H. D. Aiken. New York (1948).

THEORY OF KNOWLEDGE: containing the *Enquiry Concerning Human Understanding;* the *Abstract* and selected passages from Book I of *A Treatise of Human Nature*, ed. D. C. Yalden-Thomson (1951).

THEORY OF POLITICS: containing *A Treatise of Human Nature*, Book 3, parts 1 and 2 and thirteen of the *Essays, Moral, Political and Literary*, ed. F. Watkins (1951).

A TREATISE OF HUMAN NATURE, Book I [abridged]. In *British Empirical Philosophers*, ed. A. J. Ayer and R. Winch (1952)

—containing extracts from *An Enquiry Concerning Human Understanding.*

WRITINGS ON ECONOMICS, ed. E. Rotwein (1955).

HUME ON HUMAN NATURE AND THE UNDERSTANDING: being the complete text of *An Enquiry Concerning Human Understanding*, together with sections of *A Treatise of Human Nature, An Abstract of a Treatise of Human Nature* and two biographical documents, ed. A. Flew. New York (1962).

HUME ON RELIGION, selected and introduced by R. Wollheim (1963).

THE PHILOSOPHY OF DAVID HUME, ed. V. C. Chappell. New York (1963).

Separate Works:
Philosophical:

A TREATISE OF HUMAN NATURE (1739-40)
—Book I, *Of the Understanding;* Book II, *Of the Passions,* 2 vols. (1739); Book III, *Of Morals* (1740; 2nd edn. in 2 vols. 1817); ed. L. A. Selby-Bigge, Oxford (1888; 2nd edn. 1897); ed. A. D. Lindsay, 2 vols. (1911, rptd. 1956); paperback edition, New York (1961), Book I, ed. D. G. C. MacNabb (1962).

AN ABSTRACT OF A TREATISE ON HUMAN NATURE (1740)
—a pamphlet hitherto unknown, rptd. J. M. Keynes and P. Sraffa. Cambridge (1938).

ESSAYS MORAL AND POLITICAL. Edinburgh (1741)
—2nd edn. 2 vols, Edinburgh (1742); rptd. (4th edn.) in *Essays and Treatises,* vol. i, 1753, and in subsequent editions.

PHILOSOPHICAL ESSAYS CONCERNING HUMAN UNDERSTANDING (1748; 2nd edn. 1750)
—rptd. in *Essays and Treatises,* vol. 2, 1756 and in subsequent editions, from 1758 the title being changed to *Enquiry Concerning Human Understanding.* Ed. L. H. Selby-Bigge (1894; 2nd edn. 1902).

AN ENQUIRY CONCERNING THE PRINCIPLES OF MORALS (1751)
—rptd. in *Essays and Treatises,* Vol. 3, 1756 and in subsequent edns. Ed. L. A. Selby-Bigge (1894; 2nd edn. 1902).

POLITICAL DISCOURSES. Edinburgh (1752)
—rptd. (3rd edn.) in *Essays and Treatises,* vol. 4, 1754, and subsequent editions ed. with introduction by W. Bell Robertson (1906).

FOUR DISSERTATIONS (1757), ed. H. E. Root (1956)
—contains: *The Natural History of Religion; Of the Passions; Of Tragedy; Of the Standard of Taste.* Rptd. in *Essays and Treatises,* 3rd edn. (1760) and subsequent edns; *The Natural History of Religion,* ed. H. E. Root (1956).

TWO ESSAYS (1777)
—*Of Suicide* and *Of the Immortality of the Soul,* intended for publication with *Four Dissertations* but withdrawn. Published anonymously.

DIALOGUES CONCERNING NATURAL RELIGION (1779)
—rptd. in *Essays and Treatises,* 1788 edn; ed. N. Kemp Smith (1935;

2nd edn. 1947, rptd. New York, 1963); ed. H. D. Aiken, New York (1948; rptd. 1963).

Historical:

THE HISTORY OF GREAT BRITAIN (UNDER THE HOUSE OF STUART). 2 vols. Edinburgh (1754-7).

THE HISTORY OF ENGLAND UNDER THE HOUSE OF TUDOR. 2 vols. (1759).

THE HISTORY OF ENGLAND FROM THE INVASION OF JULIUS CAESAR TO THE ACCESSION OF HENRY VII. 2 vols. (1762).

THE HISTORY OF ENGLAND FROM THE INVASION OF JULIUS CAESAR TO THE REVOLUTION IN 1688. 8 vols. (1763)

—many further editions and abridgements were issued in the 18th century. The 1778 edn. included the author's last corrections and a short autobiography. In 1793-5 the work was re-issued in 22 volumes with a continuation to 1760 by Tobias Smollett and to 1795 by Joel Barlow. A large number of other expansions and adaptations were published throughout the following century.

Letters:

EXPOSÉ SUCCINCT DE LA CONTESTATION . . ENTRE M. HUME ET M. ROUSSEAU [Paris] (1766)

—correspondence between Hume and Rousseau relating to their famous disputation. Hume wrote the connecting passages.

PRIVATE CORRESPONDENCE . . . BETWEEN THE YEARS 1761 AND 1776 (1820).

LETTERS, ed. T. Murray. Edinburgh (1841).

LETTERS . . . TO WILLIAM STRAHAN, ed. G. Birkbeck Hill. Oxford (1888).

LETTERS, ed. J. Y. T. Greig. 2 vols. Oxford (1932).

NEW LETTERS. ed. R. Klibansky and E. C. Mossner. Oxford (1954).

Some Biographical and Critical Studies:

THE LIFE OF DAVID HUME WRITTEN BY HIMSELF (1777)

—includes Adam Smith's *Letter* to W. Strahan on Hume's last days.

AN ACCOUNT OF THE LIFE AND WRITINGS OF DAVID HUME, by T. E. Ritchie (1807).

LIFE AND CORRESPONDENCE OF DAVID HUME, by J. H. Burton. 2 vols. Edinburgh (1846).

HUME, by T. H. Huxley (1878)

—in the English Men of Letters Series.

HISTORY OF ENGLISH THOUGHT IN THE 18TH CENTURY, by L. Stephen. 3rd edn., 2 vols. (1902).

DAVID HUME, by C. J. W. Francken. Haarlem (1907).

DAVID HUME: SEIN LEBEN UND SEINE PHILOSOPHIE, von A. Thomsen. Berlin (1912).

HUME'S PLACE IN ETHICS, by E. A. Shearer. Bryn Mawr (1915).

'David Hume', by W. R. Sorley. In *A History of English Philosophy*. Cambridge (1920; rptd. 1937).

STUDIES IN THE PHILOSOPHY OF DAVID HUME, by C. W. Hendel. Princeton (1925; rptd. New York 1963).

THE ART OF HISTORY: A STUDY OF FOUR GREAT HISTORIANS OF THE XVIIITH CENTURY, by J. B. Black (1926).

DAVID HUME, LEBEN UND PHILOSOPHIE, von R. Metz. Stuttgart (1929).

'The central problem of David Hume's philosophy: an essay towards a phenomenological interpretation of the first book of the *Treatise of Human Nature*', by C. V. Salmon. In *Jahrbuch für Philosophie und phenomonologische Forschung*, Halle (1929).

FIVE TYPES OF ETHICAL THEORY, by C. D. Broad (1930).

STUDIES IN THE EIGHTEENTH CENTURY BACKGROUND OF HUME'S EMPIRICISM, by M. S. Kuypers. Minneapolis (1930).

LA CRITIQUE ET LA RELIGION CHEZ DAVID HUME, par A. Leroy. Paris (1930).

THE LIFE OF DAVID HUME, by E. G. Braham (1931).

DAVID HUME, by J. Y. T. Greig (1931).

LOCKE, BERKELEY, HUME, by Sir C. R. Morris. Oxford (1931).

DAVID HUME, by B. M. Laing (1932).

HUME'S PHILOSOPHY OF HUMAN NATURE, by J. Laird (1932).

LA FILOSOFIA DELLA ESPERIENZA DI DAVID HUME, di G. della Volpe. 2 vols. Florence (1934-5)

—vol. i, 2nd edn. with title *Hume e il genio dell' empirismo*. Florence (1939).

HUME'S THEORY OF THE UNDERSTANDING, by R. W. Church (1935).

IL PENSIERO FILOSOFICO DI DAVID HUME, di B. Magnino. Naples (1935).

THE CAUSE AND EVIDENCE OF BELIEFS: AN EXAMINATION OF HUME'S PROCEDURE, by F. C. Bayley. Mount Hermon, Mass. (1936).

STUDIES IN HUME'S ETHICS, by P. A. I. Hedenius. Uppsala (1937).

HUME'S THEORY OF KNOWLEDGE, by C. Maund (1937).

HUME AND PRESENT DAY PROBLEMS: PROCEEDINGS OF THE ARISTOTELIAN SOCIETY, Supplementary volume 18 (1939).

HUME'S PHILOSOPHY IN HIS PRINCIPAL WORK, *A Treatise of Human Nature*, AND IN HIS *Essays*, by V. Kruse. Oxford (1939).

DAVID HUME: THE MAN AND HIS SCIENCE OF MAN, by F. H. Heinemann. Paris (1940).

HUME'S THEORY OF THE EXTERNAL WORLD, by H. H. Price. Oxford (1940).

THE PHILOSOPHY OF DAVID HUME: A CRITICAL STUDY OF ITS ORIGINS AND CENTRAL DOCTRINES, by N. K. Smith (1941).

'David Hume: defender of "Nature" against "Reason"', by B. Willey. In *The Eighteenth Century Background* (1941).

'CETTE AFFAIRE INFERNALE': L'AFFAIRE J. J. ROUSSEAU—DAVID HUME, 1766, par H. Guillemin. Paris (1942).

THE FORGOTTEN HUME: LE BON DAVID, by E. C. Mossner. New York (1943).

MAN AND SOCIETY: THE SCOTTISH INQUIRY OF THE EIGHTEENTH CENTURY, by G. Bryson. Princeton (1945).

REASON AND CONDUCT IN HUME'S TREATISE, by R. M. Kydd. Oxford (1946; rptd. New York, 1964).

HUME'S THEORY OF THE PASSIONS AND OF THE MORALS: A STUDY OF BOOKS II AND III OF THE TREATISE, by A. B. Glathe. Berkeley (1950).

DAVID HUME: HIS THEORY OF KNOWLEDGE AND MORALITY, by D. G. C. MacNabb (1951).

DAVID HUME ON CRITICISM, by T. Brunius. Uppsala (1952).

HUME, SA VIE, SON OEUVRE, SA PHILOSOPHIE, par A. Cresson et G. Deleuze. Paris (1952).

HUME'S INTENTIONS, by J. A. Passmore. Cambridge (1952).

EMPIRISME ET SUBJECTIVITÉ: ESSAI SUR LA NATURE HUMAINE SELON HUME, par G. Deleuze. Paris (1953).

DAVID HUME, par A. Leroy. Paris (1953).

'David Hume', by L. Paul. In *The English Philosophers* (1953).

THE LIFE OF DAVID HUME, by E. C. Mossner (1954)
—the standard biography.

DAVID HUME, by A. H. Basson (1958).

'Hume', by F. Copleston. In *Hobbes to Hume*, Vol. V of *A History of Philosophy* (1959).

'David Hume', by F. L. Lucas. In *The Art of Living: Four Eighteenth-century Minds* (1959).

HUME, PRECURSOR OF MODERN EMPIRICISM: ANALYSIS OF HIS OPINIONS ON MEANING, METAPHYSICS, LOGIC AND MATHEMATICS, by F. Zabeeh. The Hague (1960).

HUME'S PHILOSOPHY OF BELIEF: A STUDY OF HIS FIRST INQUIRY, by A. G. N. Flew (1961).

THE MAN OF (ALMOST) INDEPENDENT MIND, by H. MacDiarmid. Edinburgh (1962).

DAVID HUME: A SYMPOSIUM, ed. D. F. Pears (1963).

THE MORAL AND POLITICAL PHILOSOPHY OF DAVID HUME, by J. B. Stewart. New York (1963).

THE MORAL PHILOSOPHY OF HUME, by R. D. Broiles. The Hague (1964).

'David Hume', by B. Willey. In *The English Moralists* (1964).

'David Hume: Reasoning and Experience', by R. Williams. In *The English Mind: Studies in the English Moralists presented to Basil Willey*, ed. H. Sykes Davies and G. Watson (1964).